THE SWANSEA I REMEMBER

The town in the 1880s and 90s

WILLIAM LOXTON

Sou'wester Books

ISBN 0 9515281 1 4

Published by Sou'wester Books (R.C. Smith)
17 Crestacre Close, Newton, Swansea SA3 4UR

Printed by Walters Printers, Clydach, Swansea.

CONTENTS

The author with his wife Lucy.

PREFACE

The Loxton family no doubt had its origins in the village of Loxton near Bridgwater, Somerset. Certainly my family came from the West of England as my great-grandfather Henry Loxton, his wife Elizabeth and young son, Charles, moved from Bristol to Swansea in the middle of the last century. No doubt like many other tradespeople they were seeking fame and fortune in the expanding industrial town. Henry and his wife were both from families associated with the boot and shoe trade, and they set up a shoe shop in High Street.

In 1866 Henry Loxton died very suddenly whilst attending a meeting in Swansea's concert hall, the Music Hall, now called the Albert Hall. His widow carried on trading at the High Street shop, but later re-married and moved to Brynamman. My grandfather, Charles, helped in the business and in 1877 married Fanny Woodroffe at St James' Church, Walter Road. They set up home in living quarters above their shoe shop at 30 College Street, Swansea. My father, William, was their eldest child and like his brother and sisters was born at College Street. William was born in June 1880 and christened at St Mary's Parish Church.

Although he doesn't mention his schooling in his memoirs, he attended Rutland Street School — this was somewhere near the present St David's Square to the south of St Mary's. Later he went to the Higher Grade School; present pupils would know it as Dynevor School.

At the turn of the century aspiring junior school teachers first worked as pupil teachers and then completed their qualifications in a Training College. My father followed this pattern and went to Trinity College, Carmarthen. His first teaching posts were in the West of England and then he returned to Swansea and taught in a school in the Hafod, eventually joining the staff of St Helen's Boys' School in 1917.

He remained on this staff until his retirement in 1943. Four years after retiring he had a serious operation, and whilst recuperating he set out these memoirs. He was bored and frustrated by his enforced inactivity when he read an article in the "Evening Post" concerning old Swansea. He commented that he too could recall the centre of the town in the 1880s and 90s, and so mother and I challenged him to write down all the tales of his childhood. He took up the challenge and spent the winter of 1947 filling three note books with his reminiscences. This book is an edited version of these memoirs.

ESME M. LOXTON
Swansea, August 1990

Acknowledgements

The publisher wishes to thank the following for their assistance with the selection of photographs: the staff of the City Archive Department; Miss Betty Nelmes (Administrator), and Dr David Painting (Hon. Curator of Photographs) of the Royal Institution of South Wales (Swansea Museum).

Thanks are also due to the following for permission to reproduce photographs: Swansea City Council, and the Council of the Royal Institution of South Wales.

"Sketty was a tiny village". This is Sketty Cross with the Bush Inn on the right.

INTRODUCTION

In the 1880s the population of Swansea was about 70,000. There were no houses in Brynmill, very few on Townhill or even Mount Pleasant. Green fields were within easy reach of the town. Sketty was a tiny village, and Sketty Road a country walk with fields and hedges on both sides.

All the surrounding districts, even Cwmbwrla and the Hafod, were isolated by open spaces from the town. Mumbles was an old world fishing village — very small but beautiful — busy only on Bank Holidays.

Swansea was a country town, where everyone knew everybody and their business. Few shops were found outside Oxford, Temple, Castle, Wind, College and High Streets. In the other main streets private houses were to be found mixed up with shops.

The Harley Street of Swansea was Northampton Place (now part of the Kingsway) which was a quiet thoroughfare, with large trees along one side and long gardens in front of each house.

Most shopkeepers lived on the premises, and there were few "company" shops.

This account is intended as a collection of actualities under various headings and refers to my earliest memories of the town. One may laugh at some of the incidents, but I can assure you that the events really did happen, and also that the conditions of life were very different from those of today.

WILLIAM LOXTON,
Swansea, Winter 1947

Sketty Road was a country walk with fields and hedges on both sides.

SMELLS

The Swansea of my childhood was a smelly country town. Most of the smells were pleasant, but a few were not very delectable. Each shop had a distinct smell: the grocer had a sweet spicy smell, and on coffee roasting days, the street was full of the aroma. One could plainly smell sheep in a gent's outfitters — proof that the wool in that shop was genuine.

The chemist definitely had a strong chemical odour, and the drapers had the dead smell of newness. Even the public houses gave a strong hint of the quality of the beer — very different from that of today. The pubs gave clay pipes to smokers free of charge, and most children had one to blow bubbles. There were four breweries in the town, and each let forth a free sample on the breeze.

The ships chandler possessed a wonderful mixture of

The West Pier, a favourite promenade, with its stout wooden railing kept gleaming with white paint.

many odours; the tallow gave pungent fumes and the freshness of new rope together with the turpentine smell of paint, almost overpowered a stranger.

The tobacconist had the pronounced perfume of real tobaccos and cigars. The coffee taverns always had the delicious odour of good, honest, wholesome cooking, and the savoury smell of the many eating houses could almost be felt. The bakers freely gave a most appetizing whiff of baked bread. Most families made their own bread; the baker supplied the tins, and baked the dough for a ha'penny per loaf, after it had been marked by means of a dinner fork with the initials of the family. The loaves, when baked, could then be claimed by the right owner. A jugful of barm obtained from the brewery was often used, instead of yeast, to make the dough rise. Bakers made little fancy stuff; they were limited to bread, cake, buns, jam tarts and sponge cakes. Every baker made a feature of real wholemeal bread — gritty stuff, but extremely filling and nourishing.

One could easily tell when "Sailors' biscuits" were being made by the ton at bakeries that made nothing else. Just inside the doorway, you could see the hot biscuits dropping from the rollers into baskets, and I often spent some pocket money upon them, at the rate of four pence per lb. Messrs Goldsworthy and Paul Smith were the two manufacturers I remember.

The Welsh flannel shops smelt strongly of tallow. A pleasant smell came from the kippers or bloaters which were being smoked at Benson's in High Street.

All these distinctive marks of trade have passed away, and now, only fish and chip shops seem to advertise on the air.

Years ago, a blind man could identify what was sold in a shop by smell alone, as soon as he came to the door. Today, one shop smells like any other.

Some other smells were not so pleasant: the tan yards of Price, and Parry and Rocke could always be located, but the worst of all must have been in the thick yellow fog, which made people cough and spit as they breathed the sulphurous fumes brought by northerly winds from the Hafod Copper Works.

Mention must also be made of the tarry fumes and the smell of new rope which filled the North Dock, and also the resinous perfume of newly sawn timber at the South Dock sawmills.

The pleasant tang of the sea was very evident when the townspeople took a walk along the West Pier — a favourite promenade.

The Pier was in first class condition with splendid seats, and the stout wooden railing was kept gleaming with white paint. The lower deck was used by anglers, and formed the abode of hundreds of rats.

Vessels waiting to load coal at the South Dock.

THE DOCKS

The docks were much busier than they are now. The North Dock was most often, quite full of ships of all sizes and types. The wharves were lined with boats, and the basins too were full up. The South Dock often had several large sailing ships, moored to buoys, lying in the middle waiting their turn at the coal hoists.

Traffic to St Thomas was much delayed by the frequent opening of the bridges. The New Cut bridge was then a sliding roadway later replaced by a swing bridge.

Boys particularly were attracted to the docks by the sailing ships. They would ask questions of the crews about cargoes, storms, where from?, whither bound?, and it generally ended up by being invited aboard to have a sailors' biscuit. Boys learnt geography, exports and imports and sometimes some language — foreign or otherwise! If one were very lucky the skipper of a small sailing vessel would let you take a pull in the ship's boat. I learnt my rowing in the North Dock. This dock was the centre of the potato and onion imports. In the Beaufort Dock were grain ships and often a large square-rigger discharging copper ore. The South Dock with its sawmills, was the home of the trim pilot boats, which were admired by everyone.

In both docks, on week-days, huge clouds of coal dust filled the air, as the coal was shot into the holds of the waiting ships. It was enchanting to watch the process, to see on the top of the hoist, the truck of coal tipping, to hear the coal grating along the shute, to listen to the banging of lumps in the hold, and to watch the cloud of black dust arise. Finally the empty truck was lowered to the quay by hydraulic pressure and shunted ready to return to the colliery.

The emptying of the water from the hydraulic pipes in the middle of the hoist, formed cascades which were a source of much fun to small boys. Many times I had a hiding for appearing at home both wet and covered in coal dust.

The one o'clock gun gave Greenwich Mean Time to the captains of the ships so that they could adjust their chronometers, and incidentally gave the townspeople the correct time.

Small trading vessels in the North Dock. (Royal Inst. of South Wales, Swansea Museum)

A horse tram, on the Gower Street to the Slip service, passes Swansea Hospital. *(Swansea City Archives Office)*

TRANSPORT

By rail, the town was linked with the rest of the country by a number of railway companies. Few train services terminated at Swansea High Street, so that passengers changed from the main line train at Landore and caught a local train into Swansea. A similar routine was necessary on an outward journey. You can imagine that this was a very unsatisfactory arrangement, especially in winter. Railway carriages were then heated by 'foot warmers' — long iron cans filled with hot water.

The London and North Western (Swansea Victoria) closed thirty years ago. It ran along the foreshore to Swansea Bay station at the Slip, then to Blackpill and Killay for Central Wales. The Midland and G.W.R. Low Level (East Dock) stations were so busy that six trains left St Thomas between 5.00 and 7.30 on a Saturday evening. These stations are long closed. Saturday was the peak day for traffic: country folk brought their produce in baskets to the market, town porters, licensed by the Corporation, wore large brass badges on their arms. On large hand trucks they conveyed the laden baskets from the stations to the market. On week days the porters carried the large leather cases of samples for commercial travellers.

In the summer paddle steamers took day trippers to Ilfracombe, Tenby and Porthcawl. Evening trips costing sixpence were very popular. Cargo vessels ran regular services to Bristol, London, Liverpool, Cork, Dublin and Glasgow and often carried passengers.

The Mumbles Train climbs the incline past Lilliput on the road from Blackpill to West Cross.

On the roads there were penny farthings, a few safety bicycles, and tricycles with two large wheels and a little one, all of which had solid rubber tyres about an inch wide. Men riders wore a cycling suit of a Norfolk jacket, knickerbockers and a sportsman's cap with two large ear flaps. The ladies, who used only tricycles, had long skirts, the hem of which was prevented from blowing about, by means of a piece of strong black elastic attached to each boot.

In the town, people who now have a car, had a horse and gig, or a governess cart and pony. The doctors each had a closed cab or brougham with a coachman in livery. Dr Humphreys who died in 1938 was the last of this type.

To reach any part of Gower, you had to travel by arrangement with a carrier, who took you in his horse bus. The passengers sat facing each other, and baskets, luggage and small boys were put on the roof, where a little rail prevented accidents. One coach station was in Plymouth Street. Some horse buses stopped at the Jeffreys Arms (replaced by the Carlton Cinema). Buses arriving from Gower on market day remained in the street all day, while the horses were rested in the Inn yard. Another terminus was in Portland Street. The horses of these buses were stabled in Bullin's Yard where Telephone House was later built next to Mount Pleasant Chapel. This was the service for North Gower.

The carriers terminated their services at their homes.

You could hire a donkey at the bottom of Newton Road, Mumbles to carry you to Langland or Caswell. (Royal Inst. of South Wales)

One served North Gower the other South. No tickets were issued, you simply paid the driver, and you had to get out and push when the bus came to a hill. Ladies, however kept their seats.

The Mumbles Railway ran from Rutland Street along the roadside to the terminus at Oystermouth called the Elms, where there was an open air roller skating rink. (The car park now occupies this site). A train consisted of a number of huge tram cars, covered workman's vans, and open cattle trucks. The latter had long benches as seats. The truck next to the engine was called the 'Dummy', because if a passenger opened his mouth to speak he would have swallowed a quantity of cinders from the loco. A train would have a symmetrical arrangement, cattle truck, workman's van, second class carriage, first class in the centre, second class, workman's van, cattle truck and then the engine. A lad sat on the front of the engine to ring a bell at the crossings.

First class carriages were always placed in the middle of the train, with the idea that the cinders and black smuts from the engine would be more likely to be received by the cattle trucks and the second class than the firsts, as each tram had open seats on top. Each tram had brakes worked by a wheel standing at either end of the platform. These brakes were necessary when the engine was moved to the front for the return journey.

A long step or narrow plank ran alongside each carriage, so that the conductors could pass along from one end of the train to the other, on the outside. Each carriage had a wooden partition across the middle — so that the running board really was a necessity for the conductors. Perhaps the partition held up the roof? At holiday times this step held many passengers who clung on as best they could. One train on a Bank Holiday would have fifteen or more carriages and carry about 3,000 passengers. Between forty and fifty thousand people were carried to Mumbles on the busiest days. The train ran hourly, and its speed can be judged from the fact that dozens of bare-footed boys entertained the passengers by 'tumbling' on the road, alongside the moving train, in the hope that they would be thrown some coins. Some boys were lucky enough to collect about one pound per day in August. The boys shouted "Throw out your rusty coppers", and "Ha'penny or a penny here".

The only tram services in the town were from Gower Street (Mount Pleasant Chapel) to the Slip, and from the bottom of High Street to Morriston and Cwmbwrla. These of course were horse drawn (they were replaced by electric trams in 1900). The Morriston trams were single decked on account of the low bridges. If a tram had to be transferred from the St Helen's section to the High Street section, it had to be drawn over the bare road of Gower St and College St, and then manoeuvred onto the lines in High Street.

Every hour, a special tram drawn by two horses, tandem fashion, left Gower Street for the Dunns, joining the Mumbles line at St Helen's junction (the Slip). It always followed the steam train to Oystermouth.

The horses for the trams were stabled at the tram sheds in St Helen's Road (where the Crown Court now stands). Boys rode the fresh horses into town, and then led the tired ones back. High St near the terminus provided plenty of manure for gardeners.

Finally one could hire a donkey with attendant, as transport to Langland or Caswell, from the Dunns for 3d or 4d. The donkeys waited in a field at the bottom of Castleton Hill (Newton Road), now shops.

There were three cab stands in the town: at Alexandra Road, Wind Street, and Mount Street (bottom of Wind Street). At each stand was a glass shelter with a stove for the cabbies.

Mumbles in 1893 — an old world fishing village.

High Street. Lewis Lewis' shop on the left.

THE SHOPS

The majority of people who lived in the centre of Swansea were small shopkeepers. When they patronised each other, most of the items were booked, and accounts were settled at intervals of six months or even twelve. As each traded with the other, settlements were easily made. For example the doctor's fees would square the tailor's account, and the boot bill would offset the grocer's account. The ironmonger would square the baker, the chemist and newspaper man would call quits, and so on. It was something like taking in each other's washing.

To obtain custom, shopkeepers readily opened credit accounts, and therefore had to have an efficient system of book-keeping. Most families had accounts for food, clothing and boots. Settlements were rarely made under a three month interval. No doubt the coming of the company shops did much to kill this system. Bad debts often ruined the small trader.

The largest drapers were Ben Evans, Lewis Lewis, Yorath, Richards the Lamb (properly the Golden Fleece), Edwards the Eagle, Philip Jenkins of the Golden Key, and Meyler. Jones the Goat, was an outfitter for officers and seamen.

The owners lived in large private houses, but the shops were not left empty at night. The assistants lived in, and were looked after by a housekeeper. The staff were strictly controlled, being fined if they stayed out late at night, or broke any of the rules of the house. Attendance at a place of worship was usually compulsory for them. Living in was in existence until the 1920s perhaps later.

The shop staff toiled long and hard from 8.30 a.m. For the first part of the week, closing time was 7.30pm. Early closing was on Thursday at 1.00, but on Friday 9.00pm was shutting up time, and on Saturdays it was 11pm. Extra duties such as clearing up, and putting up the shutters took place after closing. Most shops had heavy shutters which were stored in the cellar by day and protected the windows by night.

The chemist extracted teeth, and some had leeches for sale. These, looking like fat black slugs about two inches long, were kept in a large glass tank, shaped rather like a huge egg cup. The tank about eighteen inches across was little more than half full of water to prevent the leeches climbing out. Each chemist had an array of three huge coloured bottles in the window.

There were many saddlers on account of the large number of horses used for haulage and riding.

The only sweet shops were those of the sugar boilers. Very often, in a back street, the front room of a house would be turned into a shop. Home made toffee would be on sale with the boiled sweets. A farthing's worth was readily supplied. The tobacconist was frequently a barber as well, but there were no ladies' hairdressers. Snuff was a very popular item, and the grocer usually supplied among the groceries, one ounce of tobacco for the 'old man', price 3½d. This was a Welsh custom. The grocer provided much more raw material to the housewife than nowadays, as a great deal more food was prepared at home.

The shops I have referred to as Richards the Lamb, Edwards the Eagle etc had a carving hanging outside always painted gold. The Lamb was Mr Richard's trade

GOLDEN FLEECE—Siop-yr-Oen.

31 and 32, CASTLE STREET, SWANSEA.

JOHN & WILLIAM RICHARDS.

MANTLE & DRESSMAKING,
MILLINERY.

Linen and Woollen Drapers,

SILK MERCERS, HABERDASHERS,
HATTERS,
WHOLESALE WAREHOUSEMEN.
GLOVES, HOSIERY, RIBBONS.

MOURNING REQUISITES.

AN EXTENSIVE
TAILORING DEPARTMENT,
WITH STAFF OF
EXPERIENCED CUTTERS & WORKMEN.

ESTABLISHED 1840.

'Richards the Lamb' The golden shop sign survived well into this century outside a premises in Ystalyfera. (Swansea Guide of 1881. Royal Inst. of South Wales).

mark. No doubt, in a Welsh town, the soubriquet was useful in distinguishing one trader from another of the same name. The signs also guided shoppers who could neither read nor speak English — a common occurrence in the 1880s. English traders had to acquire enough Welsh to deal with their customers from outlying districts, or employ Welsh speaking assistants.

The trade signs I remember were:

The Dustbin	Butcher & Richards	Domestic Store
Cross Saws	Scantlebury	Ironmonger
Golden Key	Jenkins	Draper
Chest of Drawers	Moses	Furniture
Father Time & Clock	Mills	Jeweller
Civet Cat	Powlson	Toy Shop
The Gunman	Brooks	Sport
Golden Anchor	Clutterbuck	Clothier
Eagle	Edwards	Draper
Coffee Pot	Evans	Grocer
The Goat	Jones	Clothier

Flaring gas jets were used inside and outside many shops to illuminate the window display. The butchers and fishmongers in particular were lit up by rows of burners, fixed along the shop front. The first shop I remember having electric light was that of Williamson, a pork butcher in Oxford Street. In the cellar he had a dynamo driven by a gas engine. Crowds of people would collect in the street to see this wonderful new light.

Large grocers and drapers had a delivery of goods by horsevan, to a timetable for distant parts. This would be weekly, fortnightly or even monthly. The goods would have been ordered by post using a plain postcard as picture cards were not yet allowed by the G.P.O.

In the town, errand boys, would deliver goods carrying the parcels on a hand truck. Customers seldom carried their own parcels. If Father's errand boy was out on his round I would have to deliver orders which arrived late.

On Saturdays, the country folk ordered goods at the shops and expected the parcels to be taken to the station, where they would claim them. Directions would be left at the shop e.g. Davies, Glais, 6.20 Midland Station. The errand boys would be on the platform long before the stated time, each shouting the name of his shop. The rightful customer would give her name and address, to claim the parcel. One can imagine the uproar as departure time arrived and some parcels remained unclaimed. In cases where the customer came to town by horsebus or trap the parcel was delivered to the stableman at the inn.

The grocer always packed the whole order in a brown paper parcel. It was an art to arrange the various items into a compact mass, and then to tie up the package without breaking the paper. The assistants were expert at tying knots, and breaking the string with their fingers.

When a country customer wished to buy a pair of boots for one of his children, the size was rarely given. The child's age was thought to be sufficient. In most cases a piece of stick would be produced, and tried inside the boot. Few miscalculations occurred.

The same haphazard plan was adopted in an outfitters. When a new suit was required the boy's age determined the size. Hob-nailed boots were generally worn by men and boys in country districts. The cheapest men's boots sold for three shillings and sixpence per pair.

A Whit-Monday scene at the Slip. (Royal Institution of South Wales, Swansea Museum)

REFRESHMENTS

On market days thousands of visitors would require meals. For the well-to-do, the hotels were much the same as they are now. Fortunately, Swansea had a number of excellent coffee taverns, and many small eating houses. There were also faggot shops which provided cheap tasty meals of faggots and green peas.

A few pubs offered bread and cheese gratis to their clients. The coffee taverns were very popular, as they were large and very clean. In them, were long white marble topped tables, flanked by benches. Customers collected and paid for their meals at the counter before taking a place at the table. Cut rolls of bread with plenty of butter and ham or meat with enormous portions of vegetables were the favourite dishes. The meal always ended with generous helpings of rich rice pudding. Water was the usual drink with dinner. These meals were cheap and satisfying.

Near tea-time these taverns would be busy supplying the last refreshments to the ladies, while the menfolk adjourned somewhere else, to have the last one before taking the journey home.

The faggot shops seemed to be busy all day and the evening. Thruppence or fourpence would buy a good meal with potatoes. At one time, in 1894 I think, there was an automatic continental restaurant in High Street, but it did not last very long. Around a large room, with tables and chairs in the centre, were what looked like bookcases. On each little shelf, behind a glass window, was a plate with food. In one stack of shelves there were sandwiches, and in others fruit, pastries, pies, salads, bread and butter, glasses of lemonade and so on. Patrons put the correct coin in the slot, pulled a knob, and the pile of shelves moved down allowing the desired item to be removed.

Suppose a hot dinner was required, the customer placed the appropriate coin in the slot, pulled the handle which rang a bell in the kitchen below, and lo and behold on a little lift arose the meal with knife and fork, ready on a tray. If tea with bread and butter was desired, the coin was inserted, handle pulled and the tray with teapot and tea within, milk in a jug, basin of sugar, bread and butter, cup and saucer, was waiting to be taken to the table. Then the pot had only to be taken to a tap which gave forth boiling water, and the tea was soon ready. I should be safe in remarking that as things are today, the whole of the cutlery and tableware would disappear in a few days.

Oxford Street with the market of 1897 on the left.

THE MARKET HORSES

Many people came to Swansea by train and carrier, but many more came by horse and trap. The traps were parked in inn yards: The Cameron in High Street, Bullins, Castle Inn and Jeffrey's Arms. Most of the farmer's carts, gamboes or traps were left in the streets, in long lines on market day.

At the inn yards, the horses were properly stabled, but many were boarded out in the back gardens of houses. One can imagine the difficulty of leading the horse through the front door, along the passage, and out into the garden via the scullery as none of the older houses had a back entrance.

It is hard for us to realise that it was the custom for Oxford Street to be lined with farmers' carts on the market side, and that many other streets nearby had a row each side, unattended all day. The carts were piled up with the shafts of one on top of the body of the next, so as to accommodate as many as possible in the smallest space. All the streets in the area around the market and St Marys Church would be filled with carts, so that only a narrow lane was left along the middle of the street.

Some horses became so accustomed to their weekly journey that they did the trip automatically. A farmer who called habitually at certain public houses on the way home, would find that the horse would stop on its own initiative, even if its master was incapable of descending for another glass. Then after a short rest the bartender or passing farmer would just say "Gee up", and the horse would proceed to repeat the performance at the next hostelry.

I can vouch for this good horse sense: at harvest time, the daughters of the farmer at Gwenlais Fawr would drive the gambo from Pontardulais to Cwmbwrla to pick up our family, who helped with the harvest. The horse would not pass a pub without stopping, to the great annoyance of the daughters, but to the intense amusement of the visitors.

Even in the week, many farmers came to town, and would want someone to hold the horse while they did the shopping. Holding horses' heads was almost an occupation in those days.

THE MARKET

The market was on the present site but it looked very different. The vendors, each having a relatively small quantity of home produced stuff to sell, were predominantly Welsh speaking. There were hucksters as well, who did not produce, but bought in order to sell again. Nineteen out of twenty sellers were genuine country folk, and only attended on Saturday.

The dress of the farmers was distinctive. The men wore grey home spun rough woollen suits, not black, with tails, and a hat which was a kind of bowler with nearly square corners — a 'half bell topper' to a sea captain. The women wore little shawls, and their appearance was like that on picture postcards. Sorry I cannot give a precise description, but it was called 'pais a betgwn'. The takings were deposited in a large pocket tied to the waist.

Nothing was allowed to be sold in the market unless it was home grown or hand made. Two exceptions were made for china dealers and one gocer (W.J. Brown). There were many Gower butches selling home killed

Market Women. (Illustrated London News).

meat. Basket makers, wire workers, tin smiths and wood turners offered their wares for sale. At one time, a cobbler repaired boots while the customer waited — sitting on a box. Of course cockles, mussels, oysters and laverbread were popular items.

About one half of the market was under the cover of a very leaky low slate roof with large glass skylights here and there. Business was carried on in Stygian gloom even in broad daylight. The open air part of the market had detached stalls as today.

The many butchers' stalls were under the low roof which ran along the four sides. This roof which projected well over the fronts of the stalls, made their interiors very dark, but afforded some protection in bad weather. Beyond the roof were cobbled roads, about nine or ten feet wide, open to the sky. The country women stood under the shelter, but their customers on the cobbles had no protection.

In the centre of the market stood a stone clock tower and a raucous bell which warned the sellers that it was closing time — 11 p.m. on Saturdays. Buying would go on for another half hour. The people from outlying areas always left early to catch trains or horse buses.

Under the covered portion were long tables stretching from east to west. Between every two rows of tables was a long bench, upon which the dealers could sit. Home cured bacon, butter, cheese, eggs and poultry were plentiful. Customers, each armed with a silver coin, which they dug into the sample pat of butter, provided by the farmer, passed along the tables. The taste of the sample decided the sale. The butter was ready for sale in one pound pats, each stamped with an ornamental device of flowers or of a cow. It was never packed in paper, but laid on a cabbage leaf with another on top.

Small apples were sold by the count, and peas and beans by the wooden measure, gallons or half gallons. Scales and weights were too heavy to carry to market. Those used for weighing laverbread were hand scales — two pans hanging from a beam and held in the air. One stall specialised in coarse Welsh oatmeal and oatmeal cakes. Goose wings were on sale for use as hand brushes.

At Christmas time, the benches were strained to breaking point by the loads of poultry. There were no controlled prices, and customers would refrain from buying until near closing time. The farmers would sell at low prices rather than take produce home. Few deals were made without haggling. This 'beating down' was an old custom, and applied to everything sold even to laverbread, and strangely, it was usual in the footwear trade in the shops, but in no other trade. The seller raised his prices according to the attitude of the customer — psychology in the raw! When one trader had cleared his stock, the others were only too anxious to finish early, by selling for the best possible price. Many a turkey has fetched a bare seven shillings and sixpence.

It was a sight to watch the stately cocklewomen carrying on their heads, pails full of parcels bought with the proceeds of their own sales, almost running to catch the 5.15 from Victoria Station, and never was one pail seen to overbalance.

At night the lighting in the market was primitive. It was either 'bat wing' gas burners which hissed, or roaring, flaring, hanging paraffin lamps, which leaked. Each gave little light, but much noise.

As today stall holders assistants were generally family members. At about 9 p.m. on a Saturday there was a lull in sales. Prices were then reduced and selling restarted eagerly. The butchers presssed people to buy whole joints of meat at ridiculously low prices, as refrigerators had not come into use.

OUR MEAT

It was not unusual to see a flock of sheep or a herd of cattle being driven along Walter Road towards the Slaughter House in Dyfatty. The dogs had much work to do on account of the many side streets, and the drovers had a difficult task.

The animals seemed to know that the end was near. Many exciting scenes have been witnessed on the roads near Dyfatty Street, when an angry animal that had been frightened at the scent of blood, ran amok. This usually happened on winter nights. The combined efforts of several drovers, then, would be required to get the creature to the abbatoir. Until this was done, the streets in the area were almost deserted, and every door bolted.

St James' Gardens was then a fenced field, where many a flock has rested after a long journey from Gower.

The market and clock tower of 1830 were demolished in 1896 to make way for the new market which opened the following year. (Royal Inst. of South Wales, Swansea Museum)

SUNDAYS AND WORSHIP

Sunday really was the Sabbath — a day of rest for all except the housewife. She considered it her duty, first, to tog out the family in their best finery, and families in those days were large; second, to provide the meal of the week — Sunday dinner. Everything for this meal was prepared on the Saturday. The potatoes were peeled, the vegetables cleaned, and the cakes and tarts were made ready to be put in the oven. Even the joint of meat was placed ready in its roastng tin. A double lot of milk had been taken on Saturday as there was no delivery on Sunday.

While dinner was cooking, the man of the house took his brood for a walk or to a place of worship. Fathers never pushed prams like they proudly do today.

In the afternoon, the whole family would go for a walk along the Extension, this is the land between the South Dock and the sea, and thence to the West Pier. Sometimes Cwmdonkin Park would be the stroll, more particularly on a warm summer day. If the family ventured onto the sands, it was distinctly understood that it was for a walk only, as the best clothes might be spoiled, even by sitting down. Bathing or paddling must not be thought of.

The fashion parade of the upper classes was Walter Road and Cwmdonkin Park after morning service. From High Street to the Slip and beyond, was literally packed with ordinary people in the evening. Most of these came from the various chapels and churches, which were full of worshippers. Even the Albert Hall had a huge congregation Sunday after Sunday. The minister there was Rev. Oscar Snelling.

Each Sunday School was well attended by the young people. Mid-week services drew large numbers of older persons. The total number of seats in the different places of worship must have been near to that of the population.

Boys of well-to-do families were forced to wear Eton suits complete with kid gloves and mortar boards. My friends hated this garb, thank goodness I was spared this ordeal.

Certain places of worship forbade their members to go to a theatre, and those who were seen to, had to appear before the deacons. I have been told that one park-keeper used to report members of a certain chapel to the deacons, if they were seen by him in Cwmdonkin Park on the Sabbath.

In most families, reading of any popular weekly or comic on Sundays was forbidden. No dance tunes were to be played on the piano, and no songs were to be sung, only hymns were permitted. No spending was to happen, not even on a tram or on an ice-cream, and best clothes had to be worn all day long.

By the way, a curious exception to the strict keeping of the Sabbath Day, was a fair on Palm Sunday, outside Danygraig Cemetery. The road would be lined with stalls selling ginger bread, cakes, pop and sweets, and above all things Lady Teasers. It would be interesting to know the origin of this custom, as no other cemetery had such an event. I believe the fair ceased due to police objections.

Famous preachers would often visit the town. Mark Guy Pearse and Peter Mackenzie might be mentioned. Chapel members entered by the side or back door while the public crowded outside the locked gates. When the gates were opened there was a wild scramble for seats, as queues were unheard of. On one occasion I was carried into Wesley Chapel, by the tremendous crush, and my feet scarcely touched the ground. I sat in the gallery — on a step.

THE CONVERSAZIONE

One custom in our places of worship seems to have died out. The annual conversazione was a means of raising money. It might be described, somewhat facetiously, as a competitive feast. Ladies of the congregation would volunteer to prepare and equip a table for about a dozen persons, and also to sell tickets at one shilling each. Some of the tickets were unloaded on an unlucky tradesman, who would sell, use, or give them away — or lose the custom of the chapel folk.

Each lady provided her best tablecloth, china, cutlery, cakestands, decorations and silver teapot (if she had one). The event was held in the Albert Hall. Guests would walk around to look at the tables and then sit at the one offering the most delectable fare. On some tables there was solid home-made food, on others pastries bought in. One could not help noticing the competition between tables and the fight of the poor old brown teapot versus the genteel silver one.

After the tea, which lasted from 4 to 7pm, the edge of the stage was lined with the plants which had formed the decoration of the tables, and then the crockery etc was stowed away. Amidst much noise, the tables were taken away, and when the chairs had been arranged, the Grand Concert began. Why always Grand? The singers were invariably members of the choir, and an item that was bound to appear was "Sweet and low", sung out of tune.

The event always ended with the minister and officials proposing windy but hearty votes of thanks to all concerned. Then the children helped the ladies to carry home, very carefully, their crockery etc in the washing baskets.

Looking back it always seemed to me that there was a battle between the aprons of the hostesses at these events. How the lady in the rustling, black satin dress with a tiny frilled and flowered creation of an apron looked down upon the white kitchen apron which covered the skirt of another lady. And how the aspidistras on one table glared at the ferns on another! Yet the competition was good natured, and every lady did her best to entertain the guests. My preference was for the brown teapot, and the lady in the big white apron, as I always had a jolly good feed at her table.

BRYNMILL PARK

There were no houses in Brynmill, and a farm stood opposite to St Augustine's Church. The nearest houses were in Gwydr Terrace, and a few on the end of Bryn Road, on the south side. Pantygwydr House, the home of the Richardsons, was somewhere about the middle of todays Beechwood Road.

The park was usually called the 'swan park'. A stream ran outside the lower boundary. The only entrances were from Sketty Road — lined by hedges on both sides — and one well up Brynmill Lane. A miniature fair was held on Good Friday and Easter Monday, every year. The lane was lined with stalls selling the usual items — sweets, gingerbread and pop. The morning was given to model yacht racing, and later rowing boats could be hired on the lake. By the afternoon picnic parties had filled the park. On the grass, would be a large ring of people, old and young. All were expected to join in the game of 'Kiss in the Ring'. The shouting and laughter could be heard at a great distance. It was undoubtedly the noisiest and happiest throng of people in the town.

Brynmill Park — popularly known as Swan Park.

Barnum & Bailey's circus passing down Wind Street. (Royal Institution of South Wales, Swansea Museum)

AMUSEMENTS

There was no electricity so no radio or cinema. Children had to find their own entertainment.

A circus occasionally arrived at the Vetch Field. Each day, the band would lead a cavalcade of horsemen of many nations, and mounted ladies in historical costumes represented Queen Elizabeth I, Lady Godiva etc. A team of piebalds drew a huge golden throne, with a queen perched on top, and gorgeously arrayed waiting ladies at her feet. Tigers and lions in their cages, elephants, camels and the clowns all formed up in the procession. This free show was killed off by the electric trams whose overhead wires were too low.

Taylor's circus was stationed in Alexandra Road. For the last act the ring was turned into a lake.

Children's performances were given on Saturday afternoons at the Theatre Royal and The Star.

The Band of Hope was one attraction, where the members volunteered to give their little items. The Magic Lantern was a very popular entertainment; one penny was the usual fee for admission. There was a waxwork exhibition in High Street run by a Mr Fletcher. Poole's Myriorama, in the Albert Hall at Christmas, was the most popular entertainment. It was a series of large canvas pictures with powerful lights and plenty of noise behind the scenes. Turns of the Music Hall type were given between the pictures. Pepper's ghost, conjuring tricks, and acrobatic feats would be typical interludes.

But if organised entertainment was rare, there were many sources of free enjoyment. Children would listen to the patter of the many Cheap Jacks, and the Dutch Auctions held in empty shops.

Dobson's Bookshop always held a large audience, for he was a literary man, and his criticism of books was worth listening to. The highlight here was when Dobson, holding up the book would ask "Five Nights in the Bar-room" "How much?" Someone would shout "Tuppence", and in his wrath, he would order the crowd to leave, describing them as poverty stricken, ignorant and insulting. However, in a short time, returning one by one, the shop would again fill with the same crowd. Dobson would tell them that by returning, they had shown signs of penitence, and would consent to continue the sale.

Castle Street, then very narrow, was a Showman's Paradise. Children spent many evenings just listening to the barkers coaxing people to see Flying Angels, Fat ladies, Thin men, Strong men, the Bearded Lady, Performing Fleas and Sword Swallowers.

Studt's Roundabouts and shows wintered on the Strand, and attracted crowds every evening. Bunker's Hill, properly Banc Caer, was one pitch for pedlars. Others were Worcester Place, a stone mason's yard in Waterloo Street, and Quay Parade. On one or other of these places, there was someone extolling the virtues of his pills, or medicine that cured all.

The vendors were first class salesmen; their convincing chatter gave logical reasons for the bargain. Corn cures were offered by some. Pint bottles containing whole corns were exhibited, proving the cure was effective. Every corn had a history which the crowd was delighted to hear, time after time.

Mention must be made of Sequah, who sold lung tonic and embrocation. Between sales, he extracted teeth, free of charge while his brass band of Red Indians, in full regalia, blared forth horrible music, accompanied by tremendous bangs on the big drum. It was generally believed in Swansea that Sequah became Sir William Veno of Lung Tonic fame.

The oddest combination of quackery was that of a man in a wagonette who sold skin ointment, and between sales, lectured the crowd on deafness. In most cases he maintained, deafness was caused by an accumulation of wax in the inner ear, If a patient stepped up for a cure he would flourish his instrument, which looked like a lady's hairpin. In every case, a lump of wax was extracted and the ear was tested by means of a large watch. The patient swore that he was deaf before but could now hear the watch ticking. Great sensation, followed by more sales of ointment.

Crowds would be amused at the travelling potter, making household ware, while the small boy turning the wheel, would soon be covered with splashes of wet clay.

Then there was the escapologist who got himself tied up, the sailors liked this job, and would release himself once a total of one and sixpence had been thrown into the ring. The best of the street attractions for children was Punch and Judy, which was certain to be found somewhere.

In the morning, the blacksmith and wheelwright would be watched at their work by small boys, who in the evening would escort one of the bands of the Glamorgan Volunteers on its parade. One of the Volunteer battalions had a cyclists' section, which formed the nucleus of the Cyclists' Carnival. This was the parade of decorated bicycles bedecked with coloured paper, fairy lights and Chinese lanterns, and took place on a dark evening. How all the children looked forward to this pretty sight. The Hosptial Fete and Carnival arose from this.

I must not forget the Sunday School treat; the miller's carts had planks fitted across for the occasion, and the youngest members of the school would be slowly conveyed to the venue. The bigger children had to walk, but it was only as far as Sketty Hall. After tea, taken while seated on the grass, there were races and games. Then the younger children were taken back to the schoolroom to be collected by their parents. The older ones enjoyed playing 'Twos and Threes' or 'Kiss in the Ring', and a pleasant walk home in the twilight.

Old fashioned bathing machines with steps at the front, standing on four huge wheels, were kept at Trafalgar Arch. They were arranged in one long line; about fifty yards separated the gent's machines from the ladies'. As the tide went out, each machine was drawn by a horse to the waters edge, to form another line. When the tide turned, the machines were drawn back a little way to form another line. This was repeated several times until high water. The men were kept away from the female section, by a policeman carrying a cane. Mixed bathing was not allowed.

Men and boys were allowed to undress and bathe on the beach in front of Swansea Bay Station at St Helens, and hundreds took advantage of this privilege on a hot day.

Election times were exciting and provided much fun for youngsters. The boys' procession was an essential part to support one or other of the candidates. The smallest boy in the group was carried on a plank by four strong lads. The boy on the plank always had a blackened face. The other boys fell in, two by two, and the procession moved off. The little chap clung precariously to the plank as the group moved through the streets singing

Vote! Vote! Vote for Mr . . .
He's the man that we adore,
We'll hang old Mr . . . on a sour apple tree,
And he won't come to Swansea any more
Jockey Street and Johnny Street, Cwmbwrla and Waun
  Wen,
We'll all vote for Mr . . . and hope he'll win the day.

These same words seem to have been chanted in every part of the town. The candidates in a general election held their meetings in the Albert Hall. They were always well attended, and heckling and a certain amount of rowdiness was expected. Chuckers out were in readiness, and were often kept busy. I have seen them do their work very efficiently.

Torch light processions accompanied the new M.P. from the Guildhall (in Somerset Place) to his home after the result.

The Circus procession passing along Victoria Road. (Royal Institution of South Wales, Swansea Museum)

The Police fire brigade of 1882.

THE POLICE AND FIRE BRIGADE

The policeman really was the symbol of law and order. He was feared and respected at the same time. He knew everyone, and in some districts carried a cane, which was never used to my knowledge — but boys knew it was there.

As well as keeping order, the police ran the fire brigade. The words Central Fire Station were cut in the stone at the police station in Goat Street, but the only apparatus there, was a hand reel with hose pipes, stand pipes and short ladders. The steam fire pump was kept at the Section House in Lower Oxford Street. When required, it was drawn, giving out dense clouds of black smoke, by a pair of beautiful horses.

Long escape ladders, painted red, rested on brackets attached to walls in odd places away from the station, but huge heavy extending ladders on two six foot wheels, were kept ready at High Street Police Station, The Library and the Old Guildhall. It became the first duty of the ten o'clock beat, to drag these cumbersome contraptions to Alexandra Road, College Street, and Castle Square respectively, where they stood upright during the night. They were so heavy that it took the combined effort of eight men to move one of them.

Before this task was added to their duties, the ten o'clock beat marched in single file from High Street Police Station, under the watchful eye of the sergeant, to their alloted beats. High Street would be packed with people at this time, particularly on Saturdays. You could see the line of helmets twisting and turning through the crush. Reaching a corner, the last man would salute the sergeant, fall out and begin his street duty. The procession continued to their different points, and then the previous shift was relieved.

Each policeman carried a large and smoky bull's eye lantern attached to his belt, and each carried a tin can of tea. Some of the men wore beards.

As there were many drunken, disorderly and incapable nuisances, a stretcher on two wheels was the orthodox method of conveyance for them. There were regulars who had fifty or even a hundred convictions for drunkenness. There were of course a huge number of pubs and beerhouses. In the 1880s the whole borough, a lot smaller than today, had nearly four hundred. There were dozens near the market; each street had three or four. Closing time, 11 p.m., was the hour the police and respectable people feared. Whether the potency of the beer and the fresh air, or rivalry between the houses, was the cause is doubtful, but street fights were painfully frequent. Shutters over the windows of every shop were really necessary. I would not go to bed on a Saturday night unless I had seen two or three fights.

The most serious crimes of boys were the playing, in the street, of tip-cat and football. The ball was made of paper tied tightly with string. If this was confiscated by a policeman it did not matter.

As I have said the police also ran the fire service — there were no regular firemen. An old tunic and a brass helmet turned a policeman into a fireman. The brigade practice took place on Thursday afternoons at Ben Evans' store on the corner of Caer Street and Wind Street. It consisted of squirting a few jets of water, and of escapes from a second or third floor window. A few of the men assistants would volunteer to be carried down, but although the ladies were asked I do not remember any volunteering.

A canvas tube, long enough to reach the ground, was fixed to the top of the escape ladder, and a policeman would take a dive into it, to be hauled out safely at the bottom. A few bystanders would be bold enough to follow after a little persuasion, but the piéce de résistance was when the driver of the fire engine, Bobby Johns — a rather plump figure — would jump into the middle of the jumping sheet, which was stretched tightly, by the rest of the men and any bystander with a bit of weight.

There was emphasis on escape from the shops because some years before a family and their assistants, who lived in, had died when a shop in Temple Street had been gutted by fire at night. There had been serious delay in getting the escape ladders on that occasion as they were behind locked gates in the Castle Yard.

The Hospital Ball and Police Concerts were held in the Albert Hall. These were attended by the élite of the county, who arrived by carriage and pair, attended by liveried servants. Towards the end of the function, the carriages were lined up in Grove Place and Trinity Place. To call a carriage to the hall, the police would stand twenty or thirty yards apart, along the middle of the road. The M.C's. would tell the nearest man "Sir John Llewelyn's party". The message was shouted along the line, and the said carriage would proceed to the hall to collect the group. Then "Lady so and so's party" would bring another carriage and so on.

MUSIC

What would the police do today, if they found a band playing on one side of High Street, and the other side lined with interested listeners standing on the pavement? Or if they found a crowd around a one-man band blocking one of the main streets? In my youth it happened regularly and the police just smiled.

Music was heard on every day in our streets. Some of the performers were itinerant, but Swansea also boasted of regular resident musicians. Antonio, a violinist, and his partner, a harpist who sat on a camp stool, played classical music in the street. In the evening they provided the music for dances in the loft over a stable in Oxford Street.

The Town Band, seven in number, stranded here when a circus broke up, always placed their music stands on the roadside, and stood on the edge of the pavement, playing popular music. Their audience stood lining the opposite pavement.

Crowds would collect to enjoy the performances of Pony Moore, always immaculately dressed as a yachtsman. He specialised in playing two brass whistles simultaneously, and on one he was a complete master. In the summer he would take the steamer to Ilfracombe, where the crowds would boost his earnings.

On Thursday evenings, the band of the 1st (Hannay's) or of the 3rd Glamorgan Volunteers would play in Cwmdonkin Park. The Police Band was equally popular, and thousands would turn out to see them march along.

A visiting German band was formed by young men in military style uniforms. They were led by an elderly man wearing a faded frock coat. He played the big bass fiddle, with his umbrella tucked under the finger board.

The old type of barrel organ was frequently to be heard. It was a box like affair, suspended from the grinder's neck by a strap, and had one leg to support the weight. The player usually had a monkey on a long chain, trained to pick up the coppers and hand them to his owner. The large barrel organs, better described as street pianos, were beginning to be used. Each was accompanied by a smiling pair of Italians. The lady adorned in a bright, multicoloured dress, with a yellow scarf covering her hair. There was always a red jacketed monkey, canaries or budgerigars on the piano. The birds were trained to tell fortunes for one penny. One of the birds would hop onto a stick pushed into the cage, and then select with its beak, the fortune printed on a small piece of paper, from hundreds neatly arranged in an open box.

Madam Patti gave a concert every year in aid of the Hospital. She arrived at the Midland Station and was driven in an open carriage, with an escort of mounted police. She was always received by the Mayor at the Albert Hall. Once I had a hiding for being late at school. Madam's train was due at 2 pm, and school began at that time. I saw her, the hiding was worth it.

Many ships had an accordion player in the crew, and it was not unusual to hear a party of seamen, led by the accordionist, parading the streets singing shanties.

It was usual for children to learn to play the piano or violin. The teachers often knew very little, but passed on what they knew at the rate of sixpence per lesson.

The beautiful singing of parties of colliers during times of depression must not be forgotten. The men were well conducted in every way. Few picknickers returning from Gower would pass along Walter Road, without some carefree rendering of the popular songs, or more likely, of hymns. All this shows the little amount of traffic in our streets, and the latitude allowed by the police.

A helter-skelter at the Slip.

SAND

The beach was the natural attraction for the children of the town. Sandwiches and a bottle of water provided sustenance for the day. For one penny one could buy a pint bottle of pop made from Mason's extract of herbs. The cork needed to be held on by string tied to the neck of the bottle.

After an exhausting day, each child intended to take home a bucket of sand, or a small green crab in sea water. Few loads reached home, for the pavements as far as the hospital were covered in sand by the evening.

Public houses near the beach, had their floors covered in sand, but sawdust was used in the bars of town pubs.

A Sunday School outing at the Slip. A stall sells "Cooling drinks of all kinds".

The passages and ground floors of the smaller houses were flagged with stone slabs, upon which, sand was sprinkled, to give the appearance of cleanliness. Men calling "Yallow sand", or simply "Yallow", sold buckets of sand, for this purpose from flat carts.

The route of the Mayor's procession to church, was always sanded on the Sunday morning, to the great annoyance of the Sabbatarians. In the Sandfields, when there was a funeral, the neighbours, as a mark of respect, sanded the street.

Just in front of St Helens was an area of rock pools, a favourite spot for picking winkles and searching for grannie shells. High tides used to dash against the sea wall, but the sand level is eight to twelve feet higher than years ago.

On our way to the sands we looked in at the ruined Belle Vue Gardens (the Bay View stands there now), and thought of its departed glory. It had been a skating rink, surrounded by ornamental terraces and high buildings with alcoves in the Moorish style. Patrons could take refreshments there looking down on the skaters, or gaze over the bay. It was popularly called Jack's Folly. A description in a guide book of 1880 said that it had asphalte skating rinks, bowling green, billiard room, high level promenade overlooking the bay, and a commodious hotel.

SUMMER HOLIDAYS

A London journalist wrote that he did not know whether Swansea was a seaport, a manufacturing town or a holiday resort, and so decided that it was all three.

In August the town was thronged with holidaymakers, mostly Rhondda colliers. People from Swindon and Birmingham were also well represented. They took lodgings in the Sandfields, while the men of the house took pillows and slept out on the beach. The visitors would spend the whole day on the beach. Bookings were rarely made, so the rule was to arrive, and then search for accommodation. If the weather was fine, so many would arrive that the lodgings were full, and dozens of families slept on the sands surrounded by tin trunks containing their clothes.

The visitors arrived by train at High Street station and then took the St Helens tram for a penny. The platforms at either end were loaded high with their luggage. Arriving at Hospital Square, the children sat on the trunks, while the parents went in search of rooms.

The Saturday before Bank Holiday, occasionally provided pitiful scenes, especially in wet weather. Many a visitor has had to spend the night in an arm chair, or return home the same day. For a tip of sixpence, some found a few hours rest in the empty trams at the Tramway depot (the Crown Court now occupies the site).

STREET CHARACTERS

Swansea had a number of odd characters roaming the streets. Most were undesirable persons, but one was well liked by the children. He was a jolly negro, who claimed he was a freed slave. He had a happy smiling face surrounded by white hair. He always sat on a wall in Northampton Place. Though he did not beg he was offered coppers by passers by. He was getting old and tottery, and the children were attracted by his quaint speech and his merry laugh.

Jerry Russell was a public butt. He carried a stick and had a walk something like that of Charlie Chaplin. This was, no doubt, due to the amount of drink that he had consumed. He was always in a stupor, but never incapable. You must remember that the pubs were open all day.

John Leary, or Water Dog as he was called, had an enormous number of convictions for drunkenness. (Leary, a labourer living at 8 Well Street appeared before the magistrates in May 1890 charged with being drunk and disorderly in Bridge Street and assaulting P.C. Gammon (No 74). This was his forty-second conviction and he received twenty-one days with hard labour).

Ellen Sweeney had the greatest number of convictions, and was often conveyed to Goat Street Police Station on the stretcher. Sometimes she was carried on a policeman's back. Once she bit P.C. Howard's ear. He then bent down slowly and Ellen held by her wrists, did a graceful somersault, over his head, to land safely on the road. It was a real unrehearsed acrobatic feat. I shall never forget her legs in the air. (Ellen was arrested for drunkenness in Caer Street on 30 September 1890. Next day she 'adorned' the dock for the 230th time. She was told that nothing could be done for her and was jailed for one month. On going down to the cells she exclaimed "What do I care for that".)

'Lady Tichbourne', otherwise Mary Norman, was very fond of children, and when sober could not pass a child without speaking . . . But when aroused or in drink she did the most foolish things. She spent the greater part of her life doing fourteen days at a time, in H.M. Gaol, or staying in the Work-house. Inside she was known as an excellent worker. (In March 1890 Lady T received a sentence of fourteen days for being drunk and disorderly in Wind Street. It was the 76th case against her).

Now for some of Lady T's 'escapades': Commercial travellers wore top hats and frock coats. A traveller was sitting in my father's shop when Lady T. came in and demanded sixpence. Being refused she brought her fist down on the travellers topper, flattening it.

Demanding snuff from Pidsley the tobacconist at 1 College Street and being told she could have none, her fist again went into action smashing the glass topped counter.

Her most outrageous incident was on the doorstep of Thorne's, the second hand furniture dealer of 18 College Street. An armchair commode was for sale and she walked away having fulfilled a call of nature in it.

Lady Tichbourne was a frequent occupant of the 'hand ambulance'. What a thrill to be asked by a policeman to fetch the stretcher while he remained beside the 'patient'.

Jam Pot was also a public butt, with a vicious flow of

language, he could also be smelt from a distance. It was said that he had been a clown in Taylor's Circus (certainly the circus did have a clown of this name), and that he was a brother of the proprietor.

Then there was a barber called Dalling, on the Strand at the bottom of Morris Lane, who would ask for payment before starting work. When he had the tuppence, he would half do the job, and then leave the customer sitting in the chair while he enjoyed a glass of beer in the pub next door. When he had had a few drinks he would entertain his customers on the violin. Many a fight has taken place in his saloon, when an irate coal trimmer had his temper aroused by the delay. Naturally the business failed and Dalling took to busking outside pubs.

Mad Maggie (Margaret Rogers) was probably the most violent woman ever handled by the police. When she was in drink, her language was vitriolic, and her actions decidedly pugilistic. She, like all of her class, always wore a large shawl. (Margaret was sentenced to one month with hard labour in January 1890 for being found drunk and disorderly on the Strand. It was her 118th conviction. When sentenced she said to the stipendiary "You are a good sort, Mr Fowler" He replied "But you have been here 118 times". She retorted "That ain't much even if I was here 180 times". In her defence she said that she "only took two pennorth as she had palpitations very bad".

A year later she made her 130th appearance on a similar charge. "I came out yesterday after doing two months, and as I had the faceache I took a drop of whisky, and it overcome me". She was discharged with a caution.)

Sally Sawdust was a very hard worker, often employed on the potato boats in the North Dock. She bagged the potatoes and had no difficulty in carrying a hundredweight sack into town. She got her name from carrying sacks of sawdust, from the sawmills at the South Dock, to the pubs where the floors were covered with sawdust each day. She was a sister of Norris, the Town Crier. He once wrote to the Mayor asking for a new uniform. He pleaded that as he was required to accompany the Mayor to church, his Worship might feel embarrassed if the Crier looked shabby. He got his new coat.

THE OLD STREETS AND ROADS

Few towns could possibly have had such a number of narrow streets. Around the castle, every street was a bottleneck, with sufficient width to allow just one cart to pass. The pavements too were just one person wide.

Builders and painters did not seem to use extension ladders, theirs were always one piece. It would take as many as eight men to raise a ladder in a narrow street. As new buildings went up, the plans always provided for the frontage to be set back. This gave the main streets a jagged appearance of shop fronts.

Each block of houses had its own street name. For example, there were seven different names along St Helen's Road between the YMCA and the Hospital, and sixteen between College Street and the Slip.

High Street, The Cameron Arms Hotel on the right.

Castle Square viewed from Wind Street. Ben Evans' building on the left. This is the view used to paint the "Oilette" postcard which is reproduced on the front cover.

The first section of the Swansea General and Eye Hospital was opened in 1869.

Many streets had courts, reached by a narrow passage, even High Street had several. Barber's Court was the last to survive. A court contained a few small houses, all front and no back, one room up and one down. A small space in front was often a well tended garden. Most courts were blind alleys with cobbled stone paths, one tap and one communal lavatory. Bunker's Hill off College Street had six cottages.

The roads were equally unsatisfactory be the weather wet or dry. In summer the old water cart sprayed the roads to allay the dust. A cyclist would be covered from head to foot, with fine dust like dirty flour, after just a short run. Huge dust clouds, thick enough to obscure the view along the street, foretold of the approach of rain.

In wet weather, the mud was ankle deep, and had to be swept by a machine-driven brush to each side of the road. From there it was shovelled into a half cylindrical tank drawn by a horse. The mud was emptied into the North Dock. The tanks were, in later years, used by builders to carry large quantities of mortar.

Pot holes abounded, allowing pools of water to collect in the street. You must remember that ladies wore dresses which touched the ground. Streets were often flooded as the drainage was imperfect. When this happened children would float planks of wood or boxes to play as boats. Wellington Street, Beach Street and Argyle Street were often flooded, and most of the houses there had a brick threshold across the doorway.

Road mending was a major operation. The whole road was dug up by men using picks. Jagged broken stone was then spread over, and compacted by a heavy steam roller, which had to be proceeded by a man carrying a red flag — this was the law. To finish off, a pool of cement and water was brushed over the surface, to fill the spaces and bind the stones together.

Vagrants broke roadstone at the Workhouse in return for a nights lodging. One would often see a professional stonebreaker at the side of a country road. He cracked large pebbles and placed them to form low truncated pyramids at the roadside, ready for use. He would always have his food for the day tied up in a large red handkerchief. Working men usually carried their purchases in the same way.

High Street. The Palace Theatre on the left.

Ben Evans' original shop at 2 & 3 Temple Street (Esme Loxton)

ADVERTISEMENTS

It was customary for each shopkeeper to exhibit in his doorway, a selection of his stock. Some do today, but the grocer with open sacks of flour, of qualities unknown to modern housewives — leather tie, fine or superfine, cuts of bacon, and whole cheeses, showed little knowledge of hygiene, and suffered from the attention of dogs.

Butchers hung sides of beef, carcasses of mutton and pork, and bunches of lights for the cats, not only in the doorway, but also from the girder above the widow. The bookshops were decorated with books tied to long sticks, which were hooked to nails at the top of the window. Ward the furniture shop in Goat Street invariably had a bedstead standing on end outside the shop.

Rolls of material were piled in the draper's doorway, and huge rolls of flannel nearly blocked the entrance to the now extinct Welsh flannel shops. Shop windows were not dressed artistically — the general idea being to cram as much stock as possible into them.

The butcher and fishmonger plastered the entire front of their premises with meat, game and poultry each Christmas. Shoppers were attracted by the row of forty or fifty fishtail gas jets burning outside the window after dusk. At Christmas the grocer gave an almanack of a coloured picture to each customer, who, in due course, would have it framed. Weekly, tens of thousands of handbills were distributed, and several grocers issued voluminous detailed price lists.

A form of advert, now out of fashion, was a thin card, having a humerous drawing on one side, in the form of a puzzle e.g. find four children in the apple tree. By turning the card, the four faces would be found among the branches.

The Town Crier, in shabby uniform, carried a large brass bell, and was in great demand. He began by shouting "O, yez! O, yez!" and ended the announcement chiefly of sales, meetings and 'lost and found' with "God save the Queen". The crowd of listeners, mostly children, would chant "And the devil take the Crier". With bowed head, old Norris would walk slowly away, looking absolutely crestfallen.

The sandwichboardmen also had plenty of work. In groups of six to a dozen, they paraded the streets, giving out handbills and cards to passers-by. Company shops, just beginning to invade the town, generally used this form of advertisement. (J.C. Fowler, the Stipendiary magistrate fined herbalist Edward Bounds of High Street forty shillings for delivering indecent handbills to the public. The bills were distributed in High Street on 18 January 1890 by Arthur Forey. An Act introduced the previous year had deemed bills which referred to nervous debility indecent).

No chemist's was complete without the three huge coloured bottles in the window. A never failing attraction in a shop window was a working model water mill, or an endless chain of firemen running up a ladder, into the upper window of a burning house.

The widest advertisement appeal was that of the searchlight of J.S. Brown of Oxford Street, later the British Home Stores. This could be seen for many miles and was used to announce the election results by revolving in a circle or standing vertically. It was pre-arranged that the more likely result would be signalled by the revolving beam. The reinstatement of the famous 'Brothers James' (David and Evan) from the Northern Union to Swansea Rugby Club was signalled by the revolving beam, to the great joy of everyone. Was this the first news broadcast, I wonder?

The advance agent of a travelling show always left a pile of half price tickets at a school and free passes for the teachers. Sample copies of the Marvel and other ha'penny comics were given to children as they streamed out of school. Bill posting stations were numerous, and the pine end of a street was rarely without a hoarding.

The chimney sweep called out 'Hot sweep' and the chair mender called 'Any cane bottom chairs to mend'. Cockle women walked the main streets calling 'Cockles and Mussels' while carrying the pails on their heads.

A glazier with a long beard was a familiar sight. He carried sheets of glass on a frame on his back. He didn't need to call out as a broken window advertised itself.

Large firms distributed booklets, calendars, samples and testimonials of their products such as cocoa, patent medicines, Monkey brand soap and ointments. Beecham's Pills gave away sheets of thin paper to which one applied a glowing match. The message was revealed as the design burnt along the invisible printing. Most schoolchildren used a copy of 'Beecham's Book of Tables' given free by asking at a chemist.

It would be well to end this section by quoting the offer of two guineas by Usher of Heathfield Street, to the person who could find the line 'Cleanliness is next to Godliness', in the Bible. It would have been quite safe to have offered £10,000.

BEN'S

It was often said that an underground passage led from Swansea Castle to Oystermouth Castle. When Ben Evans' store was being rebuilt, hopes were raised of discovering the tunnel but the foundations revealed nothing except for the leg bones of a sheep.

The old buildings in Caer Street and Castle Bailey were two storied and each of a different design. The street was no more than twelve to fifteen feet wide. The windows were of individual pane type, some being bow windows with the large knobs of glass in some panes. In general appearance, the street frontages recalled the days of Dickens. Plate glass was fitted in the larger and newer shops. When their grand new shop was opened, Ben's employed a porter to attend to customers arriving by carriage.

TOLL GATES

The Pottery bridge and the Ha'penny Bridge carried the roads over the North Dock to the Island before crossing the New Cut of the Tawe on a further two bridges. These were under the control of the Swansea Harbour Trust and the tolls were established by Parliament. Passengers and vehicles paid a toll except on Sunday when the gates were left open. In 1890 the Corporation began payment of £3,750 per annum as compensation when the tolls were abolished.

Tolls were payable by vehicles on the main roads into the town. I remember the gates at Hafod and Cwmbwrla, where the collectors wore white aprons. I am told that there were gates on Mumbles Road near the Recreation Ground and at Uplands. I am also reminded that the Penclawdd people bringing carts to market dodged the toll by travelling via Terrace Road.

THE COMING OF THE TALKING MACHINE

The first 'talking machine' was exhibited in a shop at the High Street Arcade. Six or eight people at a time stood around a mysterious box on a stand. Thin rubber tubes, each with two ear plugs, issued from the box. The plugs were placed in the ears, the operator called for silence, and the machine was started. Amid the scratches, some talking could be heard. The speech was very indistinct, and a nasal voice announced "This is an Edison Bell Record". There would then follow a lecture on something or other.

The charge for this was thruppence a time. It was distinctly comical to look through the window, and see on the faces of the listeners, their astonishment at the invention.

Soon after this, the general public were able to buy a machine with a cylindrical record and a horn speaker.

A group of children outside a pawnbroker's in St. Mary Street. The Cross Keys Inn is on the left. (A James Andrews photo. Royal Inst. of South Wales)

HEATING AND LIGHTING

Nearly all cooking was done by means of coal or coke fires. Gas stoves were crude and unpopular, alleged to be poisonous, and expensive to run.

The coal, if bought in quantitites of more than two cwt, was dumped in a heap outside the front door. The householder had either to carry it in, or pay a man to do so. Hobblers followed the cart from the coal yard, carrying large shovels, in the hope of earning a little money.

The best Ffaldau coal cost seventeen shillings and sixpence per ton. Coke was obtained from the Gas Works, and the buyer had to provide haulage — usually a hand cart.

The kitchen range was the usual means of cooking. It was gradually replacing the open fire with oven and sham.

Only the large residences had bathrooms with hot water from a boiler. The ordinary people were content with a long galvanised bath, or the odd shaped slipper bath. These were filled with water heated on the fire — the copper used for washing clothes came in handy for this.

I have already mentioned gas lights, for electricity was a thing of the future. The gas mantles were inefficient and the air in the room became hot and foul. Ceilings were blackened in a short time and the floor of the room above felt warm. The fumes in crowded halls and chapels tended to make many people faint.

The smaller shops tended to be lit by paraffin lamps, the larger shops by gas. The streets too were lighted by gas lamps individually lighted by the lamplighter who walked around with a long pole.

Railway carriages were illuminated by oil lamps which were let down into holes in the roof. The cars on the Mumbles Railway had two oil lamps at each end, and so did the horse drawn trams.

The electric trams which replaced the horse drawn, used oil lamps to indicate front and back. Red lamps indicated the front and blue or green the rear. This was essential at night when the vehicle passed from a double track to a long stretch of single line. At the terminus the driver or conductor had to remember to change the lamps from end to end.

Tallow candles stank particularly when blown out. They were cheaper than the patent wax variety. Bedrooms were often illuminated by a candle stuck in a brass candle stick provided with a conical extinguisher. Spring grips to hold the candle had not been introduced, so that paper was used to jam the candle in the holder. I am sure this was the cause of some fires.

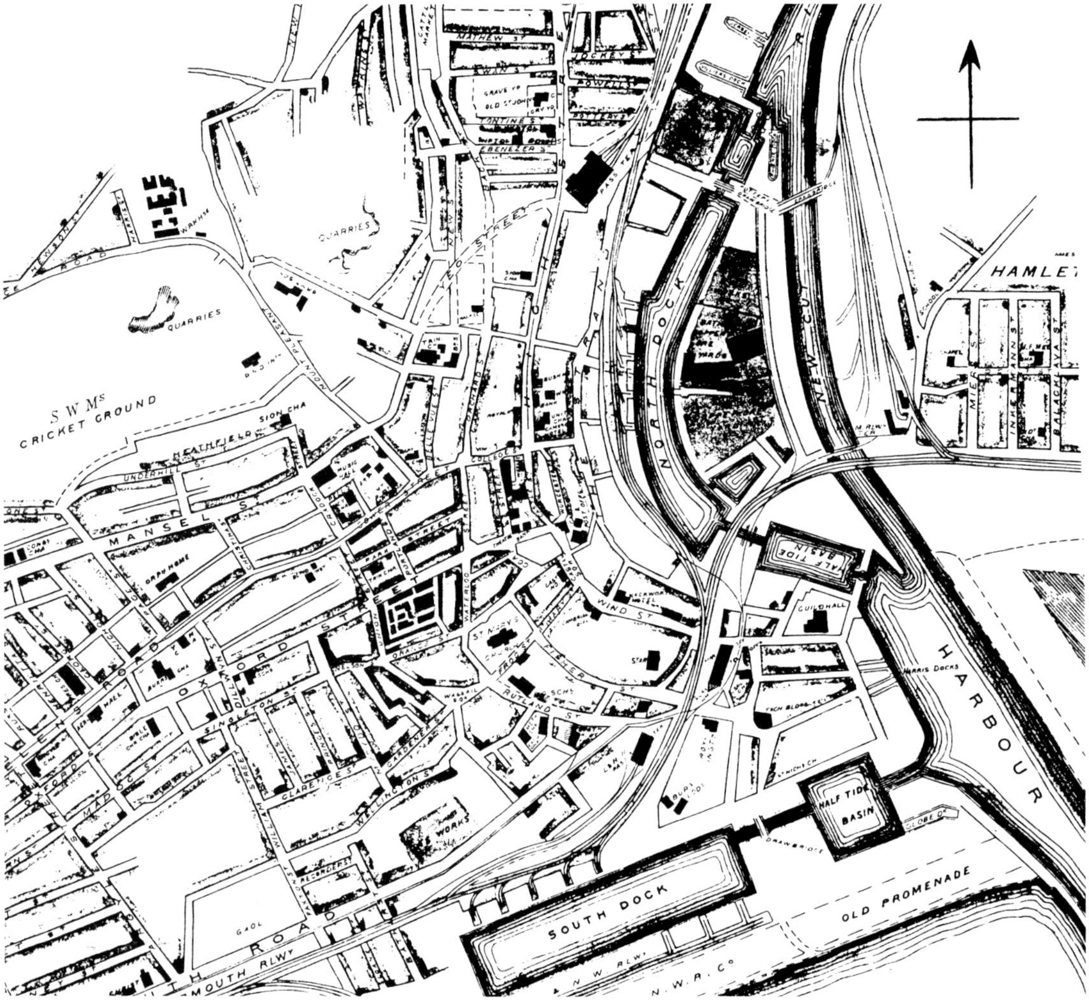

Street plan of the town centre in 1880. Prepared by T.E. Bath. (Royal Inst. of South Wales, Swansea Museum)

OLD CUSTOMS

Many traditional customs were still regularly observed, though these were by no means unique to Swansea.

A slow moving sad procession of workmen from the Hafod or Cwmbwrla would be seen carrying the body of one of their mates from the Hospital to his home. As many as fifty men took part. At intervals, the four leading men would stand aside, and wait for the bier. They would then relieve the bearers, who would fall in behind. This was repeated until the house was reached, by which time all the bearers were behind the body. It was very moving to see the reverent homage paid to the deceased.

At funerals horses wearing black plumes drew the hearse and carriages. The coachmen wore long black ribbons from their hats, or white ribbons for a child's funeral. Widows wore black mourning clothes known as 'weeds', and the children and even babies of bereaved families were dressed in black.

On New Year's Day the children observed an old custom: an orange was supported on three skewers and had dozens of wooden splinters stuck in it. The orange was held by one skewer and carried from house to house, with the child wishing the occupants a Happy New Year, and hoping for a coin. I believe this was originally of religious significance as the splinters represented the crown of thorns.

St Patrick's Day saw the members of the Irish community parading the town wearing the shamrock and their green sashes. A ball was held in the evening at St Joseph's Hall. The day began with St Joseph's Band leading a massive procession through the main streets. It was well organised by the marshalls who carried wands. The beaming priests followed the band in open carriages; behind them came thousands of silent but happy people. The men wore the shamrock and green sashes with white edges. The ladies turned out in full force wearing green ribbons on their dresses. The boys with green sashes, and girls wearing green cloaks, brought up the rear.

At the head of each group, was a huge banner, beautifully worked in vivid colours, held on two poles and four guy ropes. As rank after rank passed, in perfect formation, the pride of nationalism could be seen in the faces, and although happiness was very evident, yet there was an air of solemnity in each face.

Gower still had the Mari Llwyd. At Christmas time, the party went from farm to farm with the decorated horses head, to carry on the traditional conversation with the inhabitants.

On Hallowe'en the children played 'apple and candle', and 'nuts in water'.

THE HOME
THE FRONT DOOR

Each front door had a heavy cast iron knocker — often of a weird pattern. The sound from it was only effective in rousing the inhabitants if the door was shut.

There were no electric bells as yet, but some houses had bell pulls. The knob had to be pulled out several inches to operate the wires and levers which made the bell ring. The contraption was frequently out of order as the wires stretched and became slack with use. 'Plumbers and Bellhangers' appeared in the adverts of tradesmen.

A bootscraper was normally fitted in a little recess either side of the door. These were very necessary on account of the muddy roads.

The middle of the door was fitted with a large knob of black pottery, and a lock and bolt heavy enough to hold a ship. The key was at least five inches long and weighed near a quarter of a pound — hardly suitable for a lady's handbag.

The lady of the house took great pride in the appearance of the door step, which was whitened every day. The pavement in front of the step was well scrubbed, and decorated by a semi-circle of interlaced arcs drawn with a lump of white chalk, soft red brick or piece of free-stone. These patterns were according to the good lady's inventiveness.

Few doorsteps were complete unless there was a shining brass threshold across the step.

Tree-lined Walter Road, rather quieter than today.

THE FRONT SITTING ROOM

In most small houses, the distinguishing feature of the front sitting room was the dullness and darkness even in broad daylight, and the air seemed to be always stuffy.

The windows which rarely opened, were small with little panes of glass. The wallpaper had dull, floral designs, and the woodwork was darkly painted or stained. The idea was that light decoration would soon become soiled.

The furniture was solid and heavy. Black horse-hair covered the chairs and sofa. An armchair was certain to have an antimacassar (a covering to prevent the chair being stained by hair oil), while the inevitable what-not bedecked with small china ornaments stood in one corner of the room and a corner cupboard in the other.

The room would have a mahogany table standing on a fanciful centre leg with four sprawling feet on castors. This would be plastered with photographs and ornaments, and with an empty epergne in the centre. The mantel piece was similarly covered, but here, the chief ornament was a glass dome protecting a bunch of wax flowers. At each end of the shelf was a porcelain vase with hanging glass droppers.

Pictures and texts covered the walls. Sometimes, the legs of tables and chairs were encased in old black stockings — whether it was thought to be indecent to show bare legs, or the stockings prevented scuffing by children's shoes, I leave you to decide.

A plant, often of scented musk, or a ship in a bottle was supported on the three legged bamboo table in the window. Musk was scented in those days. Why has it lost its scent today?

This room was rarely entered except on the Lord's Day, a wedding, funeral or for a visitor. Very seldom was the fire place used, and inside the shining brass fender, lay the useless fancy poker tongs and shovel, merely for show.

In the large house with servants, the mistress could summon assistance by turning the china knob at the side of the mantel. This rang one of a dozen numbered bells in the passage outside the kitchen. The old hands knew which room to go to from the characteristic of the bell without looking at the number. They would look at the other servants and say "It's the missus again!"

THE BEDROOM

Bareboards in the bedroom, with no oilcloth, was the norm. An old rug might be placed in front of the fireplace, which was stuffed with a bag of straw. Anyhow the rug was of no practical use in that position.

The bedstead was of the black and brass variety. The best room would probably have an all brass one. Hard mattresses (straw palliases) were found in most houses. A patchwork quilt covered the bed clothes. The furniture was bound to include a marble top washstand, which was used only by the visitors. The bedroom china set had vivid floral designs, and the larger the pieces, the more it was admired. The soap holder and toothbrush box, alone, accounted for five separate pieces of china. The bedstead was draped along the sides, foot and headrail with chiffon-like material, with large bows of coloured ribbon at the end knobs and centre. The dressing table was attired in a similar manner, plus two beribboned hair-tidies.

Of course, the picture above the head of the bed, and the one over the mantel piece, also was adorned with more muslin and ribbon.

The mantel board always had a deep fringe with tassels fastened by large brass-headed nails, and the iron-work was hidden by two draped curtains, edged with bobbing.

No bedroom was complete without the framed texts, and a beautiful mahogany chest of drawers — probably a family heirloom.

The Library in Alexandra Road was opened by Gladstone in 1887.

GAMES

The basis of children's games was very little material at small cost. A wooden hoop and a skipping rope with painted wooden handles were essentials for a girl. Open spaces or quiet streets were required for play. Of course all the streets had slow moving and infrequent traffic. Hoops were bowled along the road and girls formed large parties for skipping with a rope across the road. Every girl could perform several styles of skipping, and good-natured competition was usual. Cross Street near St Mary's Church was a favourite place for skipping and the ever popular 'hop scotch'.

For a boy, a whip top, a peg top and an iron hoop were the usual requirements. A pig's bladder, at a cost of tuppence, made an excellent football. A visit to the Slaughter House at Dyfatty was necessary for this purchase. Cricket was occasionally played at a lamp post, but tennis was out of the question.

Marbles were carried by all boys and the terms bratching, fulucking and knuckling were known to all. Frog Street was the popular marbles venue. Pedestrians had to walk in the road as the footpath on the church side was occupied by scores of boys involved in a game. By the way bratched meant that one had lost all ones marbles in a game, knuckling was shooting the marble by means of the thumb while the knuckles rested on the ground, and fulucking was an unfair form of knuckling — jerking the hand towards the target while shooting.

Spinning a peg top is a forgotten art these days as is the skill of racing with whip tops.

Tip-cat or cat and dog was a rather dangerous game, which often ended in the Police Court, or in a collection to pay for a broken window. It involved striking a pointed wooden peg, the cat, with a club known as the dog.

LEISURE

In the evening, or when it was raining, a girl would be busily employed in the house, or by cutting out and making clothes for her dolls. The doll was often nothing more than a 'sally' or wooden clothes peg. Time never seemed to drag as there was so much to do. Boys and girls made miles of corkwork, which was then formed into table mats.

A boy with a magic lantern was greatly envied. A steam engine powered by meths, or a clockwork toy would be taken to pieces, and carefully cleaned and oiled before reassembly.

The science and art of making and flying a kite was fully explored and every boy was an expert in sharpening and using (or misusing) his penknife.

When it came to writing, pen and ink and paper were in second place to slates and pencils which allowed vast amounts of fun at almost no cost.

Juvenile literature had not developed; you had the ha'penny comic or the old fashioned story with the obvious moral lesson. The 'Deadwood Dick' type of adventure existed, but in most homes it was absolutely forbidden. The lurid picture on the cover being sufficient for the ban. The *Christian Herald* and *Tit Bits* were read in most homes, but the latter was not to be read on Sundays.

The library seemed to care little for the young reader,

and one was fobbed off with any old thing by a grumpy old chap called Salter. There was no junior section as today and most of the books were in very poor condition. Parents ordered the grubbiest books to be returned immediately for fear of catching fever!

Nearly every child had to go through the agony of learning to play a musical instrument. After half an hours practice one was free for the rest of the day.

On fine days, exploratory excursions were made to Town Hill (then fields and farms), Kilvey, Clyne, Sketty or Cockett. The return journey was always made by a different route to add to the sense of adventure. On Mount Pleasant Hill there were some houses and the Grammar School but plenty of large green fields could be reached in five minutes from the town. As I have said before most of our spare time and holidays were spent on the sands.

The reading room of the Library.

SATURDAY NIGHTS

At weekends, the streets were crowded from the afternoon until late into the evening — something like Oxford Street of today. There was little horse traffic after tea-time. At the eleven p.m. closing time groups of men would gather outside the pubs to continue the arguments which had begun at the bar. The arguments often ended in fights with the crowd obligingly making a ring around the combatants. Both men were likely to be drunk, and so the fight seldom lasted very long. The policemen, always good natured, stopped the fights by their very presence and would allow the rivals to be parted and led away by their friends.

There was some dangerous fighting when the Militia men, who were training in the town, took off their heavy leather belts, each with a heavy brass buckle, and swung them around their heads. By mid-night the streets were very quiet and the rats took possession of the gutters. Buckets and boxes of refuse were placed in the doorway at night for the early morning collection by the scavengers. This was a boon to the rats as bins with lids had not been introduced.

FETCHING THE DOCTOR

An amusing incident occurred when a child was born in our street. Granny Morgan, the midwife, was sent for at two in the morning, and her husband was asked to fetch Dr D.A. Davies of Northampton Place.

On pulling the bell at the Doctor's house, Morgan was startled by a voice alongside him saying "Who is it?' and "What do you want?"

Mr Morgan started to run away and, looking over his shoulder, saw the house in darkness and no other person. Being a matter of urgency he plucked up courage and returned to pull the bell once more. The doctor had guessed that the caller was frightened, and told him not to be and to step near the bell pull and to tell him what he wanted. Morgan did so and the doctor duly dressed and attended the birth.

The next time that Morgan was sent to fetch the doctor he knew how to use the speaking tube!

A LUCKY ESCAPE

I must have been very young when I was playing with the snow which had been shovelled off the pavement forming a heap alongside the kerb. The snowfall had been heavy and pedestrians were walking in the middle of the road, because of the danger from roof-falls.

Our building was three-storied. A. G.W.R. wagon was turning the corner when Wedlake, the driver, noticed that the snow on the roof above me was beginning to slide, so he cracked the whip to frighten me, and I jumped back inside the shop.

Just then the snow crashed down covering two men who were knocked down. One of the men, a solicitor named Norton, was badly hurt. His box hat had lessened the blow from the iron guttering which had struck him. He was in hospital for many weeks and brought an action for £1,000 against my father. Luckily a receipt was produced showing that the premises had been painted and the shoots repaired, only a few months before. As reasonable care had been taken the action was dismissed with costs.

SWEETS AND ANGELS

Austin, a sugar boiler, kept shop at 29 College Street and Mrs P . . . a toy shop at No 27. Hard-boiled sweets cost four pence per pound. The old lady purchased one penny worth of sweets each week at Austin's. She would taste a sample taken from a tray on the counter and declare it unsuitable. "Not that sort Mr Austin". One after another each variety was tasted and found wanting. She then sampled the sweets in the row of bottles on the shelf behind the counter.

At last she would find a sort to suit her palate and, putting a penny on the counter, would say "I'll have a penn'orth of these Mr Austin."

Mr Austin stood this game for some weeks, but then made up his mind to stop this sharp practice. The next week, after the selection had been made in the usual way, he picked up the penny, put two sweets into a bag, twisted the paper professionally, and announced "This, madam, with what you have eaten, makes one penn'orth". Mrs P . . . took her valued custom elsewhere.

Some years later Austin gave up the sweet shop, and began a business as a bird fancier. He became well known for training a parrot which sang the first verse of the popular song "White wings, they never grow weary". Many children were late for school by listening to the bird whose cage was hung in the window above the shop. Goat Street has been blocked many times by crowds of listeners. I swear that the parrot did the singing, but in the light of the next tale, I sometimes wonder how it was done. This shop had a tablet on the front, indicating that Beau Nash was born there. In later years it formed part of Sidney Heath's premises.

In his spare time Austin ran a show in Castle Street, emblazoned with an enormous canvas picture of an angel — large enough to cover the entire shop front. He acted as his own barker and cashier, and holding a huge scimitar, would invite the public to see the actual Flying Angel — admission only one penny. When a sufficient number had paid, the curtain was drawn to reveal the Angel flying in the back of the shop.

Austin flourished the sword in all directions around the angel who thus appeared to be quite unsupported. The angel was in fact Austin's son aged five or six, draped in white and with wings fixed to his back. A harness suspended him from a heavy iron girder hidden in the roof. The back cloth was of black velvet, and the lighting dim. There seemed to be no shortage of people willing to pay for the privilege of viewing the Flying Angel.